LOTUS EYES
LOTUS FEET

LOTUS EYES
LOTUS FEET

Poems by

INDRA ARMSTRONG

Please try to listen
  The sights beyond our eyes,
Shine bright and glisten
  In brilliant golden skies;
Not within our vision
  Yet open to our sight,
It's not on television
  But still shines on at night.

GANAPATI PRESS

Cover painting by Jennifer Armstrong.
(Chintamani)

For further information, please write:
Ganapati Press
1344 Pacific Avenue
4 Palomar Arcade, Box 142
Santa Cruz, California 95060

DEDICATION

These poems are dedicated to the memory of my beloved spiritual master His Divine Grace A.C. Bhaktivedanta Swami Prabhupada. He appeared like the full moon amidst the firefly philosophers of this dark age. If any truth shines in my words it is merely a small reflection of his grace; any faults are my own. I would also like to thank: Patita Udarana (who encouraged me), Hari Hara (who believed me), Kanupriya (who was a friend), Keshava (who listened), Tarun Kanti (who was a brother), Mangalananda (who sang them), Paul Uszcienski (who lived them), a certain Ph.D. (who wanted them), and lastly my wife Chintamani and daughter Shakuntala (who are the real poets although I move the pen).

OM TAT SAT

CONTENTS

shri saraswati

LOTUS EYES
LOTUS FEET

PROTOPLASMIC CRUD

Well his parents both were monkeys
Who had crawled out of the mud,
He was simply made of matter
And protoplasmic crud

Formed by sub-atomic bumping
In a random sort of way,
With no goal and no direction
Simply animated clay.

Made complete by evolution
He finally learned to walk,
But though nothing needed saying
He somehow learned to talk.

And he built a vast dominion
In which each thing had a use,
Saying, "All this leads to nothing
Life's a complicated ruse."

Then he gave himself a title,
Made himself a PhD,
Gave himself the job of teaching
This insane philosophy.

Though he claims we're going nowhere
We are told that we should hurry,
And though we're only chemicals
The chemicals still worry.

But now science has the answer
To the problems of our race,
They've made billion dollar rockets
To bring rocks from outer space.

Yes, their ancestors were cavemen
And they've shown it through the ages,
By their inability
To listen to the sages.

Now the answer to this riddle
Should they ever care to hear it,
Is that matter cannot move
Until it's touched by spirit.

But it's hard to teach a monkey
The things he cannot feel,
And it's hard to show a caveman
What's beyond his cave is real;

But the hardest thing of all
Is showing the absurdity,
Of claiming life's an accident
To men with no humility.

PARTHENOGENESIS

You've heard of Adam,
He discovered the atom
As he tried to relieve
A lady named Eve,
With a weakness for snakes
And a couple bad breaks;
So they cut down the trees
And bought color TV's,
Polluted the skies
Built a new paradise.
With a crane they were able
And a wrinkle-free label
Hoping not to die,
Bought insurance from a guy
With a crew cut and a grin
Who smelled of original sin;
And the accidental babies
Raised on formula and maybe's,
Read the bible science fiction
Saw the moon shot resurrection,
But could see what they were gettin'
Was a brand X Armageddon,
With a nuclear conclusion,
To the fission in the fusion.
Had they thought the prophets meant
The money should be spent?
And forgot the words of Moses
Who felt bad and sent roses,
To the funeral of a race
In the depths of outer space,
On a planet that will glisten
With the proof it wouldn't listen
Till the flood will come again,
Then another group of men
Try to live but not to harden,
In the cosmic kindergarten.

PLASTICATED ELASTICITY

Caught in our complicity
Complicated modern thought,
Thoughtless of simplicity
Simply made of what we bought.
Bought, but with duplicity,
Duplication lead to naught,
Naughty electricity
Electrifying all we sought.
Sought no elasticity
Elasticated, over-wrought,
Wrought by our plasticity
Plasticated and distraught.
Distraught by vulcanicity
Vulcanistic force we fought,
Fought for our veracity
Verified that we are caught.

EGYPT

Rapidly advancing man,
Stop the wheel, if but you can.
With progress made of stone and steel,
Such monuments are surely real;
Time no doubt has closed its eyes
And sleeps in this new paradise.
Disease is sick and soon will die,
Then death will perish by and by.
We'll change the moon, and reach the stars,
And spend our days in motor cars.
Unwanted life we must abort
To free our time for better sport—
Avoid the losers, they grow old,
The puritan ethic and the common cold;
We must give up discrimination
In automated liberation—
Lined in rows or stacked in boxes,
Breathing air with fumes obnoxious
Fruit trees dying, grass all brown,
But don't let progress get you down,
It's "better living through chemistry"
A man-made, plastic, eternity.

MOTHER MURDER

While you were deep inside your mother
Waiting for the gift of life,
How would you have felt, my brother,
When you saw the surgeon's knife?

Secure, and sure that she was kind,
Protected there within her womb,
What kind of thoughts would cross your mind,
Betrayed and slaughtered in that tomb?

Without a struggle or a fight,
Disposed of like some strange disease,
If you had never seen daylight
Would you be living as you please?

For out of sight is out of mind,
And you may think that none can see,
But in your heart, the judge will find
You guilty of murder, first degree.

HARDCORE

O X ray'ted
Physical science,
Mutated
Self-reliance,
Pornographic
Heartless robot,
Waiting in traffic
'S what you got.
Thanks! doctor,
For the pill,
Head "proctor"
Of baby kill.
Your brain is
Really great,
A kid whiz
At disintegrate.
Progress, O
Plastic suit,
Who'll go
To your debut?
Wasteland
Of cosmic fire,
Trash-canned
Earthly funeral pyre.
Yes, thank-you
(Mr. Rational)
For a brand new
International—
Growing scientific
Quasi-coalition,
Of non-specific
Deadly demolition.
Yes, history
Will remember you
As a mystery,
The remaining few
Will spend their days
Cleaning up your mess,
'Midst the lingering rays
Of your tenderness.

TEST TUBE BABY

He was made inside a test tube
In a lab at M.I.T.,
By a biophysics major
Working on his PhD.

On a dark and windy evening
As the scholar tinkered late,
He stumbled on the secret
Which began to percolate.

In a mild saline solution
With a slight electric charge,
The hydrogen and carbon
Started somehow to enlarge.

And day to day he watched it
With a moist maternal eye,
Supplying bottled oxygen
So the foetus wouldn't die.

While lying in the hormones
From a hundred chimpanzees,
The child developed nicely
With no problem from disease.

On a digital computer
That cost three hundred grand,
The pregnancy was normal
As the scientist had planned.

And soon the day arrived
For the opening of the tank,
The doctor took the baby out
And gave it the usual spank.

Then he handed him to the student,
And I'm sure you know the rest,
He began to feed it formula
From an artificial breast.

Yes, the pregnancy went smoothly,
Though the birth was rather odd,
But science is making progress
In imitating God.

TRAFFIC TOLL

The cutting wheel
Of your progressive—
Thoughts should feel
Their roll repressive
Crushing life,
The traffic rolls,
Heedless knife,
The gentle souls
Lie bleeding
(By the way)
Are you heeding
What I say?
Slow down
Your own demise.

GREAT WHITE DOCTOR

With words you've made yourself respectable,
Antiseptics keep the odor undetectable.
Those titles make you so impressive,
Your plans for life are all progressive—
Great white doctor to the rescue
With the chemicals to cure what ails you.
Been tested on the useless monkeys,
Nature kindly made to be your flunkeys.
Taught to use the scalpel by the helpless creatures,
Who acted as your most unwilling teachers,
Killing life, you hope to learn to save it.

DEADUCATION

Pedantic
Epidemic,
Academic
Epileptic,
Perspicaciously
Professorial;
Edifyingly
Colloquial.
Profane
The profound,
Pass it around,
Give it to
The nation;
Call it education,
Teach it in
The schools,
Certificated fools
Sniffing every
Sentence,
Dogs, with a
License.

WHAT'S YOUR PROGRAM

O noble guardians of the truth,
You'd like to save the foolish youth
From the hopeless legions of the damned,
They'll thank you when they're deprogrammed.
In the name of love, with a lot of cash,
You want to save the youth so rash.
Smoking, drinking, radio blaring,
Your every seventh word is swearing;
And driving up in a Cadillac,
You've come to bring your baby back.
Because you love your child so much,
You signed him over to such and such—
Who's only in it for the money,
The things he does will not be funny,
But all that matters anyway
Is what he teaches your child to say.
To somehow get him back to normal,
It's just a little old-fashioned informal,
Neo-Nazi gestapo technique
Like the one you saw on T.V. last week,
On your favorite sex and violence show—
But where did freedom of religion go?
And why don't you try to deprogram
The members of the Ku Klux Klan?

AUTOMATE

Modern science (while improving life)
Finally invented the greatest machine,
A lightweight aluminum mechanical wife
To raise the kids, to cook and clean.

No monthly breakdowns plague this model
With plastic hair, no need to comb,
No emotions to cope with, tears to coddle,
And programmed never to leave the home.

Our artificial insemination kit
Takes the guesswork out of pregnancy,
Choose a he or she or it
With a money-back safe delivery.

No fits of anger, temper or moods,
Trained only to flatter and compliment,
We're proud of the large well-mannered broods
Our mothers can raise in a tenement.

And one last feature we know you'll love,
our newest model includes (of course)
Soft plastic skin that fits like a glove,
And an all fees paid "Las Vegas" divorce.

DR. FROG, PhD.

Doctor Frog was a great professor,
A genuine PhD.,
Who lived in a pool in a shallow well,
Just as happy as he could be.

He'd measured the sides to the top
Of the section that he could see,
And then written books on the universe
By thinking inductively.

"There's nothing beyond our inspection,"
He would say with finality,
"It's conclusive truth we accept a priori—
In relativity."

But then came that fateful day,
When a frog who had been to the sea,
Descended within their tiny pool
And spoke with great subtlety:

"I've come from the shore of the ocean
In a land of infinity,
The water there is inconceivably deep
And exists for eternity."

"What's that, you say?" said the scholar.
"I doubt your veracity,
You say that this place is as big as my well,
Is it one time, or two times, or three?"

And croaking he puffed up his airsac
In proportionate quantity,
And he kept on inflating it bigger and bigger,
Expanding it arrogantly.

"Is it ten times or a hundred?"
He said, in anxiety,
Only moments before his bubble burst,
And he passed on immediately.

So the point of this story is simple,
The professor's mentality,
Could not understand what was outside his well,
And he gave up his PhD.

Yes Dr. Frog was a brilliant scholar,
A little like you and me,
Who didn't believe anything was real,
Except what he could see.

RE/PRO GRESS

So busy making progress,
We forget to wonder why,
Life started in the first place
And why we're born and die.

Surrounded by the gadgets
That we're told will save the day,
We still get old and perish
But why we cannot say.

Now gardening and fruit trees
Will soon be obsolete,
And instant food from factories
Is what we'll learn to eat.

For man can make inventions
But he can't invent the Truth,
And all his vain pretensions
Won't restore his youth.

While our scholars seek solutions
In the rubble of the past,
Poking ancient mummies
To find out how to last.

And ruled by foolish leaders
Who play with us as stakes,
Our world is being ruined
By mad scientists' mistakes.

But man has made great progress
So they'd like us to believe,
It's measured by the ugly mess
Our children will receive.

Yes progress marches onward
But don't you think it's odd,
How forward looks like backward
And no one mentions God?

JUDAS GOAT

Well I've listened to all the leaders talk,
Seen how they'd rather ride than walk,
And heard them give the cons and pros
Of things that everybody knows.
Their speeches made of but and and,
Where no one really takes a stand,
Are liked by those who wish to cheat
Or someday win themselves a seat.
I've seen them fighting needless wars
Behind the safety of locked doors,
While thousands gave their lives in vain
As they enjoyed the stolen gain.
I've watched them moving men in herds
With shepherds speaking clever words,
For nothing more than love of power,
I've seen them making good men cower;
And forcing the children to waste their youth,
They teach them mere words in the name of truth,
While their mothers dance naked to pay the rent
To the landlord who owns the tenement.
Yes I listened so long that I almost lost sight,
Of the meaning of words like justice and right.

EASY MONEY

Let not the sleep of ignorance creep in,
Your heart will find no shelter in the night
Where darkness hides the empire of sin,
The pleasure of those souls who fear the light.

Beware the flattering promises of men
Whose eyes betray the meaning of their speech,
Before you follow, ask them where they've been,
And find out if they live the things they teach.

Be careful when they talk of easy gain
But never seem to tell you of the price,
Their carelessness is easy to explain,
So when you go to follow them think twice.

Take heed that you may see the waiting trap,
For fools rush in where wise men never tread,
They'll smile and put your head upon their lap
But only you will suffer when you're dead.

UGRA KARMA

The more things that you take
The less you have to give,
The more hearts that you break
The less you'll want to live.

And every cruel deed
Will follow you for years,
An unremembered seed
Which grows up into tears.

And the night will not protect you
Or conceal a hidden sin,
The evil that you do
Is witnessed from within.

Is it worth the price you pay,
That fleeting moment's gain
Which, in another day,
Will only give you pain?

Are you wandering across the earth
With no thought of times to come?
Have you thought of your next birth,
And all the things you've done?

TRICK WORLD

Mad world
Bad world
Running after sin.

Sick world
Trick world
Someone did you in.

Mean world
Green world
Dying with a grin.

Old world
Cold world
Where did it begin?

Poor world
Sore world
From the constant din.

Dark world
Hark world
To the voice within.

REFLECTIONS

I started out unborn,
And birth reminded me
I had forgotten my name
Was picked out randomly,
From several carefully
Designed coincidences
And ran into the unknown
Late one night—
In fear that my reflection
Was not really me.
Beside my self I sensed
Another pair of eyes
Behind my own,
(A million dreams)
Like distant echoes
In the universe,
My mind unseen
Awaited times unfolding;
Darkness swallowed up
My fragrant youth,
For it was never really mine.

POLISHED ANIMAL

I have served my wicked masters
Toiling for them night and day,
Standing in line to be cheated
My life has been stolen away.

The endless drudging march of life
Drags me in its jostling throng,
Oppressed by bags of bulging flesh
I somehow limp along.

And my days are lived to eat
Then hide away in sleep at night,
A grunting pig in a fancy pen
I never see the morning light.

My pleasure ground is a perfumed bag
Of mucous, skin, bones and air,
All painted up to look alive
I spend my evenings there.

And my specialty is causing pain
To satisfy my endless lust.

DOUBLE ENTENDRE

O I have lived on, through death's
Dark hold, like passing breaths
Through space in painful repetition,
Falling into dark perdition;
Glimpsing heaven's beauties far above,
Looking through my eyes, for love
That never could be there,
A double entendre—

And missing the point,
I get the joke, a joint
Like this, what's a girl,
A sad neglected pearl
Such as yourself doing herein,
And that rhymes with sin
Which in passing let me say
Is why we have to stay—

O give me rest my words
Are frightened cat chased birds,
And eaten by the dark
The day is like a lark—
On the wing,
Hear it sing,
Such a subtle soulful song
Be careful not to listen long
Or your heart will grow wings,
And other such unheard of things
Will take away your stolen pride,
And then where will you hide?

PAIN GEOMETRY

These hard lines
Hurt my heart,
Right angles all wrong.
Squares rule my life.
Parallel lines,
End in frustration.
Boxes are obnoxious.
Wrecked-angles,
Lead me on—
To peer-amidst
The circumlocution.
O bleak
Lines drag on,
Beyond the point
The pair relax,
And spy release
In inner space—
Taking the "G"
Out of "Om" it tree,
Of life unbound;
Ground, it up
And out of line—
Planely speaking
I want out.

NOT SO MERRY GO ROUND

I have seen a million deaths
And yet I still live on,
I've had a million parting breaths
But I was never gone;

Played so many parts that I
Cannot tell who is me,
But none of them could make me die
I live eternally.

I think therefore I am is wrong
I am therefore I think,
But where in life do I belong
What is the missing link?

I'm lost and nowhere to be found
And yet I still exist,
I'm miserable and wandering 'round
And yet I still persist—

Upon the ferris wheel of life
Unable to get out,
Entangled in a web of strife
A prisoner of my doubt.

O DOCTOR

Each day my condition is worse.
Hunger returns with the morning.
Everything I eat becomes waste.
My eyes look but see not enough.
Even the birds pierce my ears
Crying in fear as they fly.
The tongue in my mouth is a tyrant;
Two nostrils his wicked ministers,
Tease his angry wife, the stomach,
Who flirts with his commander, the genitals,
Court poet for hire,
My obsequious mind, pays them court.
Foolish jester, my dwarfish tongue,
Dances with lunatic riddles.
Each night my wealth is robbed
By the clever burglar sleep.
Disease demands the taxes
Beyond what I can pay;
And pain the police, beats me daily.
The city is crowded with desires,
They all talk at once in my head.
O Doctor, please do something quickly,
I'll give you whatever I own,
Just cure me of having this body,
And stop it from killing my soul.

MY MISCONCEPTION

I was born
Into a land
Confusion,
Conceived of chaos
In delusion
(By mistake)
My mother
Left me lying
In the street;
And playing there
I met deceit,
A clever dog
And other friends
(Like greed and anger)
Lust, would have me
Taste the drink
Of liquid fire,
Rising up from
Carnal contact, and desire
Became my
Constant companion,
Like bad dreams
Falling into a canyon,
But never hitting bottom
(Only falling)
So much pain in life
I started calling,
Out to God.
(Even though they told me not to)

THE TRIAL

Across the endless universe,
Each star's a witness shining bright,
Who testifies to man, the judge,
With perfect evidence of light.

Presenting countless legal points,
The lawyers vice and virtue rage
Within the courtroom of man's mind,
Exchanging views from age to age.

It seems that there has been a crime
For all who live are forced to die,
The room is silent, tense and grave;
The jury must discover why.

They call the moon and then the sun,
Who take the stand for all to see,
Destroying darkness with their rays,
They argue for eternity.

But still the judge would have more proof,
Although the verdict is quite clear,
That light will always conquer dark,
The accused is ordered to appear.

And so the bailiff's voice rings out,
"Will God please take the stand,
For He must now explain Himself,
And answer this high court's demand.

He must appear to clear things up,
And solve this complicated case,
He has no choice for He's on trial
For murdering the human race."

Again they called, but no one came,
Next day the morning papers read:
"The case of 'God vs. Man' is closed;"
The verdict was that "God is dead."

ONE NOTHING

If life came from out of darkness,
Then who made the light of the sun?
If there really aren't any,
Then who is everyone?

If something is actually nothing,
Then how could it weigh a ton?
If we're finally going nowhere,
Then why don't we walk and not run?

If there's nothing to gain by our living,
Then what will we have when we're done?
If the Ultimate Truth is nothing,
Then how can I be one?

PAYDAY

Some say
To play
Today
Away
Just may
Defray
The day
We pay.
I pray
That they
(So gay)
Will stay
That way
When grey
They lay
And repay
Earth's clay,
The delay
Can't defray—
Judgement day.

YOU'ALL

When I say
I, addressing you,
Implying we,
Including they,
Assuming us, the
I which we
Assume is us, is
Part of that
Which he, she
It, include
Within themselves.
That, from which this
They has come,
Is also there,
(Where they therein)
Are who indeed
They are.
And yet as they
(He, she or it) are
In and from that,
We can see that
(In that) there
Is they and we,
And I mean that
When I say
I to you.

PLEASE LISTEN

I want to tell you a secret of life
When all is said and done,
You have to pay back all the debts
You owe to everyone.

I'd like to save you a lot of trouble
Protect you from the pain,
We suffer in our ignorance
Thinking we are sane.

(Between you and I) it's a long way to go,
But what else can we do?
For life doesn't stop, and even death
Is the start of something new.

It's hard for me to tell you this
Because of life's confusion,
But we have to learn to see beyond
The trap of our illusion.

I only wanted to point this out
Because we're all the same,
We have to learn what life's about
And get a higher aim.

NOTHING DOING

All this talk about nothing
Is really something,
If you know what I mean;
Nothing to say,
So why write
Books of meaningless words?
Just try to imagine
A library with nothing
But books upon the void,
When you've read them all
You disappear!
But before you go,
You write a book about it
He or she,
What to speak of me—
All are gone.
Nobody is writing again,
Sitting on the chair,
Pretending nothing's there
Long enough to write it down,
It's very tricky,
This "nobody" somebody
Saying "something" nothing
To "no one" everyone
With his "unmanifest"
Manifest hand.
You heard me right,
Words are useless.
(That's right I heard you.)
No that's not it.
Well what is it?
No not that:
It is not
That it is not,
Not not, that it is—
Is and is not not.
Not not
Is, and is not;
Not not not, is
And is not not.

Would you repeat "that
Which is not" once more
So I can miss it again?
Especially the end,
The part where you disappear.
Now you see it,
Now you don't.
It all comes out in the wash.
Everything is
A big mistake;
I'm only teaching
(That you don't need teachers)
And saying
(You don't need words)
Are you catching on?
Then let go,
It's a word,
(It's insane)
It's the void!

GROWING OLD GRACEFULLY

When I was young I learned
That I was growing old,
And knowing that, I yearned
To speed the process on.
Then looking for examples
Of people who had aged
Successfully, it seemed
That they were all engaged
(I never would have dreamed)
In mad pursuit of youth.
The bathrooms were their temples,
While mirrors offered proof
That time cannot be slowed
Or made to hurry up;
And though they were bestowed
With what I sought to gain,
They wished to stop the clock
And live the past again.
"If that's the case," I thought,
"Their words cannot be true,
The lessons I've been taught
Are things they do not do."
So in those days I tried
To learn the reason why,
My elders often lied
And never wished to die.
"There's something funny here,"
(I thought and think it still)
"For all grow old, it's clear,
While youth is what they will.
No doubt this is a riddle,
Not just another view,
A point of great importance"
(And though I was quite little)
I finally got a clue,
A rumour in my school,
Once whispered after class
By one most thought a fool,
That "Life is like a looking glass

And not what it would seem,
The body dies, but soul
Lives on." It was a beam
Of light that brought a goal,
Which time cannot destroy.
My teachers never heard
(Or else could not enjoy)
The beauty of his word.
They said it was a rhyme
That scientists thought odd,
From prehistoric times
When man believed in God.

THE SCENE

Well when I saw you see me see you,
I could see you saw me too,
And though we saw the same thing,
I still was me and you were you.
Although the thing we saw was common,
It appeared as something new,
Because we saw that seeing it,
Was something both of us could do.
I had not seen that you were seeing,
(Seeing only what I saw)
But seeing you was seeing something
Seeing something I had seen.
This seemed to clear the whole thing up,
Until we saw that we were being seen
Before we saw each other seeing,
And now I saw that seeing was a scene—
Set up by Someone who was watching,
Seeing who would see that He could see
That what we saw was seen before we saw it,
And that seer, seen, and seeing, make it three.
The things were there to see before we saw them,
Which proves that Someone always seeing saw—
Long before we ever sought to see Him;
And even seeing said that sight had seen,
For what we saw was seen with sight and seeing.

SONGBIRD

My soul is like a nightingale
That's singing in the dark,
And waiting for the sun to rise.
My heart is like a lark,
That's winging through eternity
With melancholy notes,
A song in search of love that's real
Throughout the heavens floats;
A melody of loneliness
Composed in ancient time,
And sung by all who fly alone
The lonely songbird's searching rhyme.

RESCUING HAND

O small that I am and humbled
By the slavery of anger and lust,
I walked on my own Lord, but stumbled,
And come to You now with my trust.

In a land filled with rivers of tears,
I passed my childhood and youth
Trying to live with my fears,
But I come to You now for the Truth.

This bondage to matter is endless,
Like children who play in the sand
We stand on the seashore defenseless,
Except for Your rescuing hand.

Deluded by flickering pleasure,
I was lashed by the whips cold and hot,
And all of my searches for treasure
Turned out to be that which is not.

BAD BARGAIN

My heart is like a pawnshop,
Where people buy and sell
The things they never needed,
But always kept so well.

Stacked upon the dusty shelves
In sad neglect they lie,
Like strange forgotten memories
Of dreams that wouldn't die.

I'm only a second-hand merchant,
Trading in others' pain,
Taking much more than I'm giving,
But never content with my gain.

And my business was purchased with money
I received from the sale of my soul,
In a moment of rash speculation
With no thought of the Ultimate Goal.

O dear Lord, You alone can release me,
For there's nothing You're looking to buy;
Only Your mercy can pay off my debts,
And only Your love can teach me to cry.

LOST LORD

O Lord, I only measure You,
Why can't I learn to treasure You?
Night lasts all day long.
Darkness follows wrong.
I never learned to pray,
And went the other way.
My eyes refuse to cry,
A voice keeps asking why,
While selfish doubt
Locks mercy out.
This winter age is cold,
My life was bought and sold—
To feed my face,
I lost Your grace,
And kissed the lips of death.
Each wasted breath
Refused to say Your name,
I shrink beneath the shame,
And bend to sin
Again and again.
O, please take back a child
Out crying in the wild.

CAUSELESS MERCY

I saw the light
Coming down from the face,
Of the beautiful Lord
Far beyond outer space.

So radiant and bright
Shining perfectly clear,
Descending in glory
And removing all fear.

Once in the night
I did wander in pain,
Praying for sunrise
To see him again.

Then from great height
Came a vision of grace,
Pure causeless mercy
From a transcendent place.

Well I know it is right
When I see Him so near,
In the sky of my heart
In my eye as a tear.

O, grant me my sight,
Let me stand in the rain,
Of Your rainbow of love—
The eternal refrain.

DELIGHT THE RIGHT

If your eye is bright,
You will touch with light.
If your strength is right,
You will win the fight.
If your deeds are white,
You will change your plight.
If you sing His might,
You will reach great height.
If you have His sight,
You will conquer night.

ARETIST

O, have you heard the laughter
Play beneath the ancient bows,
Of silver trees with hair of gold
Where lovers made their vows;

Or watched the clouds downpouring
And felt that raindrops all are tears,
Have you ever lived a moment
For a hundred thousand years?

Then perhaps you've seen a sunrise
Shining like a brilliant eye,
Or felt the moon embracing you
From high up in the sky.

You might have even noticed
The dewdrop diamonds on the green,
If you've been watching carefully
All this you must have seen.

And if you never blinked
You must have seen the artist's hand,
Painting slowly with His brush
Upon the canvas land.

LOST AT SEA

I pray, O Lord, my heart is Yours
While traveling near lonely shores,
Where monsters wait and dragons sleep,
And dreams of wickedness are deep.
Within the night the tossing waves
Pound the moaning buried graves
Of lost and crying souls, my Lord
This ocean is so deep to ford.
And howling winds, the snake of time
Has captured me as waters climb
In crushing peaks above my head;
My mind is weak, my body dead.
My soul is wandering in the night
When suddenly I see a light,
A beam beneath the thundering clouds
That drape the dreadful sky like shrouds.
Above the rushing foamy strand
I see a rock in splendor stand,
And anchored firmly at its height,
A lighthouse with its beacon bright.
But like no light I've ever seen,
It glows so radiant and serene
Amidst the terrors of the dark,
And guides my torn and battered bark.
That light then cuts a lucent swath,
Through ignorance so black, a path
Bright hope shines forth amid the reefs,
Of hate and endless bleak beliefs.
But Lord, is this some conjurer's trick?
How can light stand in dark so thick?
Or have you finally sent Your grace,
To save me from this hopeless place?
I pray, O Lord, my heart is true,
That I may someday come to you,
And reach the distant ocean's shore,
To live with You forevermore.
I pray O Lord, my heart is Yours,
While traveling near distant shores.

OUT OF THE BLUE

Listen to the music of the morning,
The gentle voices whispering in the night,
Among the trees
The humming bees
Are singing songs of harmony and light.

Ocean waves are pounding out a rhythm,
The moon conducts a symphony sublime,
The stars that shine
Each sing a line
And all the planets dance to keep in time.

Mountains sit in silent meditation,
The faces in the clouds go floating by,
And drops of rain
A cool refrain
Teach everyone the art of how to cry.

Sunshine touches all of us with kindness,
The rainbows arching softly in the blue,
And winging birds
Like subtle words
Each part of nature offers us a clue.

Laughter rolls throughout the sky like thunder,
The wise men bow their heads, and smiling nod,
For nature's grace
Reflects the face,
And all the wondrous beauty that is God.

CAN'T CHANT

The blessed chant.
The stubborn shan't
The clever bant
The angry rant
The crooked slant—
The ignorant
The rich implant
The poor supplant
The hungry pant
(The rest say can't)
The blessed chant.

GOOD-BYE MAYA

O Maya you are smiling,
Casting your enchanting glance
Dancing an alluring dance,
My gentle heart beguiling.

For years I've been your lover,
Meeting you in secret places
Seeing your eyes in myriad faces,
I never loved another.

But loves and lovers come and go,
As winter takes summer's rose
And coldly her soft petals blows,
Across the white uncaring snow.

Yes Maya dear, I've found another,
Lotus-eyed Govinda perhaps you've met,
For hearing His name your eyes are wet
With the tears of a childless mother.

WHAT NOT

O I am not
A water pot
Nor image made of earth,
I'm not an it
Or just a bit
Of something with no worth.

And emptyness
Does not impress
Me as a happy place,
I'd be remis
To have no bliss
And really miss my face.

I'm not a thing
Nor everything
And can't be everywhere,
To end up gone
Would lead me on
Which hardly would be fair.

I'm not just one
Or just begun
How could I have an end?
To be a that
Would leave me flat
I'd rather be a blend.

But most of all
Although I'm small
I'd really miss my Lord,
Without His love
And life above
I really would be bored.

EKANTIN

Shining bright in every eye, playing gently
Teasing beams of, laughing lightly
Hidden faces, winking out the wordless
Sprightly smiling message, who would guess
The hidden manifest, an open secret
Sees, reflected seeing myriad mirrors it.
Spinning circles, atoms dancing, merrily
Warbling this, the songbirds ecstasy
Trilling, up the high empirean dome,
Circles of the seventh heaven roam;
And search in silence the dauntless night,
The topless depths, and bottomless height
Within the flower petal maze of fragrance,
Drunk with beauty, drunk with but a glance.
Again the sweetest well out-rushing,
Sweeping sleeping life, with gushing
Beauty hushing in the timeless deeps,
And dropping seeps, within each cell it leaps,
But living life, the secret keeps within,
Pretending to be hidden on the skin,
Brightly shines the image day and night,
The hidden Lord, within our seeing, out of sight.

LOOK THIS WAY

O Govinda of unsurpassable splendor,
Bowing my head I turn to You and surrender
Far from the worldly noise, the lonely confusion,
Past the passing of time and matter's illusion.

O Gopala most kind and radiant master,
Please hear my song and help me come to You faster,
Holding my heart in my hands I bow down completely,
Now appear in my mind and speak to me sweetly.

O Sri Krishna with eyes like a lotus flower,
Playing Your flute in the shade of a bamboo bower
Far from this world of death and endless pain,
Please cast your glance and give me life again.

A CHANGE OF HEART

The caterpillar changed his mind
And woke to find himself refined,
His old self had to die
For him to be a butterfly.
He tired of walking on the ground
And so around himself he wound,
A screen of silken strands,
A veil untouched by human hands.
Then something subtle changed within,
Reflected by his changing skin,
He had a change of heart
And wished to play another part.
If like that worm my soul can fly
A rainbow colored butterfly,
Upon the winds of time
Then I with wings of gold will climb--
Beyond this burning dark abyss
Up to that land of love and bliss,
Where grows a flower sweet,
I'll fly to Krishna's lotus feet.
And there I'll live eternally,
My soul at last from matter free
A song will fill the sky,
The lovesong of a butterfly.

GURU

O I am poor of heart,
A wandering beggar I,
Bereft of common sense
Do cheat and steal and lie.

My evil thoughts and deeds,
Swarm like angry flies,
Lay their sticky eggs
Upon my mind, then die.

But though I wander lost,
And full deserve my fate,
You've come to pay the cost
Before it is too late.

Dear Prabhupada, you bring
Sweet music to my life,
Who else but you can sing
Amidst the death and strife?

Who else can show the way;
Lead me from the night?
Your golden moonlike ray
Has given back my sight.

You danced within my heart,
Where no one ever came,
Loved me from the start
And sang the holy name.

Your voice is filled with love,
It stirs my sleeping soul,
Your singing fills the night
Within this wretched hole.

So I am yours eternally
I trembling hold your hand,
I'll serve you all my life,
With love we'll leave this land.

A SIGN OF SURRENDER

O cold mechanic desert life
I'm not your child you're not my wife,
Nor will I wear your dusty clothes
I feel the thorn, I've smelt the rose.

Outworn my shoes are growing thin
From trackless miles of wandering sin,
In lands where only cactus grows,
I feel the thorn, I've smelt the rose.

O long the night, and short the day
How cruel December, fragrant May
Was always short and filled with foes,
I feel the thorn, I've smelt the rose.

On Himalayan silent peaks
I sat for years and months and weeks,
Retreating from your painful blows,
I feel the thorn, I've smelt the rose.

In countless births I've vainly sought
Escape from death but I was caught,
Within a trap which I had chose,
I feel the thorn, I've smelt the rose.

So many times the moon rose high,
And filled with light the darkened sky
Yet I my foolish eyes would close,
I feel the thorn, I've smelt the rose.

And every time the dawn appeared
Its light reveal that which I feared,
A land of death beseiged with woes,
I feel the thorn, I've smelt the rose.

The mighty ocean rolls and swells,
Its depths enclose our private hells
But no one all the secrets knows,
I feel the thorn, I've smelt the rose.

Now finally Lord I hear Your song
I'll see you soon, it won't take long
No more Your love will I oppose,
I feel the thorn, I've smelt the rose.

So let my every word and deed
Be free of anger lust and greed,
For each man's heart his action shows
I feel the thorn, I've smelt the rose.

O let my chanting fill the skies
So love for You may fill my eyes,
Let serving You be my repose
I feel the thorn, I've smelt the rose.

PATITA PAVANA

O I have kissed the feet
Of every woman in town,
Cast aside my mother sweet
And dragged my father down.

The list of my sins is carved
On the faces of all I see,
Whose fearful hearts are starved
For knowledge, bliss and eternity.

But O the spiritual master pure
Your divine grace Srila Prabhupada,
You've come to save us who are poor
By bringing deathless love of God.

So fallen I lie on the ground
Homeless I sleep in the street,
And crying do wait for the sound
Of your voice or your lotus feet.

BECAUSE BECAUSE

Govinda is the Cause
Of all causes,
Because
He has no other cause.
Being Himself causeless,
He causes
Causelessly,
Causing causelessly
Just because,
His cause
Is the original Cause.
Cause causing
Cause because,
His cause
Is the original Cause,
And there is no other cause
Beyond His causing cause.

A.C. — ALWAYS CHANT

His divine
Grace A.C.
Bhaktivedanta
Swami,
Has saved us
Who fell
From the darkness
Of Hell.
Prabhupada
Gave us life,
Sang of God
In the strife,
With a voice
Filled with love
Brought a choice
From above;
In a song
Full of bliss
Singing long
For the kiss,
Of our sweet
Loving Lord,
Touch his feet
Climb aboard,
Dance and sing
Chant the name,
Hear it ring
In the sky,
Chant forever
Never die.

COMPLETELY COMPLETE

The Personality of Godhead
Is complete,
And concrete,
Him I greet
At His feet,
Cruel death obsolete
Only He can defeat—
Any feat
None can cheat
Him, or beat
Him deplete
Or delete
Him, replete
And discrete
My heart beat
Does entreat
Him, complete,
I repeat
That a seat
Near His feet,
Which secrete
Nectar sweet
Makes complete
Life's repeat;
And complete
Love's complete
Life's complete
Is complete.

VYASA PUJA

O Prabhupada I touch your lotus feet
And yearn to taste that nectar which is sweet,
As humming bees to fragrant flowers fly
Or restless lovers watch the evening sky,
So I am always thinking of your grace
And meditating on your moonlike face,
Which shinking rose to brighten Kali's night,
That gentle glance which gave me back my sight.
And who bestows his mercy on us all
Forgiving us those sins which caused our fall?
To you jagat guru I give my heart
And humbly praying that we never part,
I honour you on this most holy day,
O most beloved Abhay Charan De.

NARAYANA

Behind the veil of sense perception
Past the echoing halls of time,
Beyond the realm of self-deception
Exists a vision so sublime,

A truth transcending all illusion
The resting place and dearmost friend,
Above the fetters of delusion
Without beginning middle or end.

The eternal Lord and primeval One,
The final goal and support of all,
The source of the moon stars and sun
The place from which we chose to fall;

As pearls are strung upon a string
And seem to hang in empty space,
On Him is resting everything
In Him is standing every place.

He is the life of all that be
The only master of time and death,
And the cost of this vision of ecstasy
Is the price of giving your living breath.

BRIGHT HIGH FLIGHT

Eternal master lead us through the night
Your footprints in the sky,
Will never die
Or vanish from our sight.
We follow you as soaring eagles fly
Above the mountains' height
We seek the light,
Beyond the Sun on high
Where lies the spirit worlds in splendor bright;
The tears you cry,
Our broken hearts unite
And sailing in the mercy ship you ply,
We fight the only fight
For what is right,
And change our darkened souls from black to white.

NATURE'S SECRET

The interplay of dark and light
Caused the birth of day and night,
As changing seasons come and go,
From summer rain to winter snow—
The dance of spring and death of fall
By force decree the fate of all.

But who has formed these lucent beams
Which, touching darkness, fashion dreams?
Who has painted evening dark,
Made the laws of nature stark?
What mind conceived the crimson rose
Whose fragrance on soft vespers blows?

A thoughtful mind would contemplate,
To learn the ways of One so great;
But claiming all we see as ours
And heedless of the passing hours,
We waste our lives in foolish games,
Entangled in a world of names,
And lost because of our false pride
We cannot hear the Lord inside.

He's standing there within our heart
The Whole of Whom we are a part,
But only through the loving grace
Of he who looks upon His face,
Will we again be blessed to see
His beauty and His majesty.

RAIN OF MERCY

Just as a thunder cloud pours rain
Upon the forests burning plain,
So you your rain of mercy send
Upon devotee flowers who bend—
And gently sway upon a breeze,
Their fragrance offered at your knees.
The breeze is soft and gently sighs
The holy name 'neath summer skies,
Reflections of Your loveliness
Upon their budding consciousness.
While black bees humming gather 'round
To taste the nectar of the sound—
You speak the silver moonbeams dance
And fall beneath your loving glance.
O Prabhupada wandering free
Through Vraja's fields in ecstasy,
Please place your feet upon my mind
O lead me father I am blind,
But when I hear your soothing voice
I feel my burning heart rejoice.

HEARING AND CHANTING

Quietly, lest we should be overheard
Or understood without the proper heart,
Ring forth our voices with the sacred word,
A holy act for those who will take part.

Think not that truth is captured by your speech
Nor fall within the letters' clever spell,
Stand tall and raise your arms their greatest reach
But never grasping, wait beside the well.

In silence try to hear the gentle voice
Yet always active keep your weapon sharp,
Lament not evil nor the good rejoice
Your mouth speak music sweeter than the harp.

With kindness for the innocent, the child
Compassion for the suffering and weak,
Like lightning strong, yet like a rose bud mild
While always mindful of the end you seek.

Detached, but always working for a goal
Austere, but never harsh in food and drink,
Controlling mind and body with the soul
Aware that senses do as heart did think;

And mind receives its orders from the ear
Who listens to the stories of the tongue,
Then speak that only which is true and dear,
Your life will be the songs which you have sung.

So sing the endless beauties of the One
Whose hair is dark and curls about His face,
Who sits upon a lotus in the sun
With eyes more deep and blue than endless space;

Who lives within a garden in the breast
With loving friends who gayly gather 'round,
In radiant glowing garments He is dressed
My words fall flat and pray upon the ground.

Embrace His feet, O heart bejeweled with tears,
Surrender, rise, and dance to see Him smile,
Give up the pride that burned you all these years,
His love was waiting for you all the while.

Sing songs that thrilling, fill the waiting skies,
Rise on the wind, this song, O Lord of Light—
Descend to the souls of the gentle and the wise,
Rise up like the glorious Sun dispelling night.

KRISHNA SUN

Shadows dance before my eyes they
Touch me in the light of half-day,
Teasing me with sweet distraction
Formed of light's sublime refraction.
Whispering secret innuendo
Dazzling colors like a rainbow,
In the sky of my desire
Kindle in my mind a fire;
Maya calls me to her chamber
It's her duty who can blame her.
Prabhupada I hold your feet so
Though I see her I will not go,
And I watch the pale horizon
Straining to the East with eyes on—
Rosy hues of dawn's arrival,
Birds of love the days' approach call,
Cries my heart, I hear Him coming
Dancing smiling flutesong humming.
Lord I am a morning flower
In' Your servant's window bower,
He has grown me for Your pleasure
Planted in my heart a treasure,
And You as the Sun are rising
All the darkened world surprising:
Hare Krishna Hare Krishna
Krishna Krishna Hare Hare
Hare Rama Hare Rama
Rama Rama Hare Hare.

O GOVINDA

O Lord the Sun's effulgence hides Your face
The darkness of the night conceals Your eyes,
Your hands and legs reach all through outer space,
And dawn displays Your beauty in the skies.

The rainbow shows the colors of Your dress
The movements of the Moon reflect Your mind,
Your smiling is the cause of happiness
And love exists because You are so kind.

The rolling rivers flow forth from Your veins
The clouds that fill the sky come from Your hair,
The seeds of life are watered by Your rains
And from Your breathing blows the mighty air.

My Lord You are the source of all I see
Your movements are the passing days of time,
You are the resting place of all that be
And loving You has made my life sublime.

O Govinda within my heart
Celestial herdsman lotus-eyed One,
Your precious gift of love impart
O You Who stand behind the Sun.

THE BIRTH OF BLISS

O listen gentle souls please hear us sing
With joyful hearts a message we bring,
Of he who came to save us from disgrace,
Our beloved Prabhupada, His divine grace.

The sky was filled with flowers on that day
When he appeared Abhay Charan De,
His lotus feet this fallen world would grace,
Our last chance, His divine grace.

Lost we are and searching in the night
Praying in darkness give us our sight,
O turn toward us divine and moonlike face,
Smile and show the way, His divine grace.

Now countless sins are burning in our heart
We fallen souls from the Lord did depart,
Only you can save the human race,
Fall at your feet, His divine grace.

Chaitanya's mercy you came chanting Hari Nama
Blessing all with prema, instead of deadly kama,
O purify our hearts leave not a trace,
O lord and master, His divine grace.

The Absolute Truth has lotus feet you said
What a gift, we thought that He was dead,
Such sweetness you brought to this terrible place,
Fall at your feet, His divine grace.

So simple and clean, truthful and pure
Devotional service alone shall endure,
Your message has given a life full of brace,
Serve at your feet, His divine grace.

O dear Prabhupada hear your children sing
Your message in every village will ring,
Service to Krishna through your loving grace,
Serve you forever, His divine grace.

GOKULA

Above the din
The roar,
The sound within
is more,
To be heard
Like a dream,
Or a bird
It would seem,
To be what
It is not
Something but
Not a lot.
Gentle voice
In your heart,
Eternal choice
You are part,
Of the whole
Mystery,
Give your soul
And be free.
When you know
Who you are,
He will show
You His star,
Where each walk
Is a dance,
And they talk
With a glance,
From sparkling eyes
Shining with light,
Of endless surprise
And innocent delight.

DIVINE GRACE

With your perfect vision you opened my eyes,
And touched my sleeping soul
In its hidden place,
With your loving grace,
I was broken, but you made me whole.

Just when the clouds were filling the skies,
And keeping me from the light
I was fading away,
With nothing to say,
But you came and restored my sight.

Like the full moon shining bright on the rise,
You appeared in the sky of my heart
O the heavens rejoice,
At the sound of your voice,
And all ignorance has to depart.

Dear master, your words of wisdom so wise,
Have been sent by the Lord from above
To enlighten all men,
And teach them again,
The way of eternal love.

GANGA

Graceful, sparkling, crystal water
Youthful, storm cloud's lovely daughter.
Mountain mother; endless giver
Surging as the wind has taught her.
Bride of life, enchanting river,
Misty garments veil her graces
Swirling whirlpools, smiling faces
Graceful leaping diamond falls
Her necklace, rainbows, hidden places;
Caves like festive wedding halls.
Running with the spotted deer,
Maids of honour, rushing streams
Weeping willows bending near,
Blushing where the ocean gleams
She waves to see her husband dear.

WHITE ISLAND

There is a distant place called Sweta-dwipa,
Where lying down in silent cosmic sleep,
Surrounded by a milky ocean white
Within a castle on an island bright,
The universal Lord sweet smiling dreams
And from His moonlike face soft lucent beams—
Shine forth revealing gold and silver halls
Green emeralds, rubies, carven ivory halls—
Where endless rows of pillars formed of pearl
Are swept by towering ocean waves that curl,
And toss their foamy nectar all through space
Gold earrings decorate His smiling face.
A flower garland rests upon His chest
In silken yellow garments He is dressed,
With blackish hair that curls about His ears
His lotus petal eyes remove all fears.
Complexion blackish like a thunder cloud
His graceful form with four strong arms endowed,
Is resting on a soft white serpent bed
With pointed tongues and fearsome eyes of red—
A thousand headed snake with bluish scales
Is coiling far beyond this world of veils,
And lying there Narayana casts His glance
Across the endless miles of ignorance.
He enters in the heart of all that be
Each golden sunbeam shows His majesty,
His holy name is filled with nectar sweet
And purest love flows from His lotus feet.

NAUGHTY BOY DAMODAR

Naughty boy Damodar bound by ropes,
The knot will hold, Your mother hopes,
But only You know what You've done—
She loves You more than anyone.

A chubby blue baby with restless eyes,
And soft pink feet, caught by surprise,
Naughty boy Damodar bound by ropes
The knot will hold, Your mother hopes.

You stole her butter and ran to play,
Fed the monkeys then hid away
In a lonely spot with a frightened face,
But she found You and then began the race—

Faster and faster Your mother ran after,
Naughty boy Damodar shaking with laughter,
Finally is caught, but the rope is too short
By inches she's missed You what lovely sport!

Naughty boy Damodar bound by ropes,
The knot will hold, Your mother hopes.
She's got You now You naughty boy.
So You'll have to stay and give us joy.

With fetters of love she has You tied,
Strengthened by the tears You cried,
For ropes are one day torn apart
But bonds of love are in the heart.

Naughty boy Damodar bound by ropes,
The knot will hold, Your mother hopes,
But only You know what You've done;
She loves You more than anyone.

ACME OF ENTITY

The fountain of youth, beauty and Truth,
Dressed in garments of yellow silk,
Lives in Vrindavana where rivers of milk
Overflood the land at the sound of His flute.

The Cause of all causes and Primeval Lord,
His smiling face, the king of all moons,
Eternally sports in lotus lagoons
With nothing to do but dance and sing.

The Master of mystics and source of all
In the form of a blackish cowherd boy,
Plays with His friends in pastimes of joy
And their laughing and joking floods the land.

GOVINDAM

I offer my most respectful obeisances unto the Absolute Truth,
Eternally present in His abode in the form of eternal youth.
I worship Govinda the primeval Lord, the first progenitor Who
Is tending the cows yielding all desire, His complexion heavenly blue.
Like a blackish cloud, with a peacock feather rainbow on His head;
And a flute in His hands, His blooming eyes like lotus petals spread,
In the land of spiritual gems, surrounded by millions of purpose trees,
And always served by hundreds and thousands of Laxmis or Gopis.
Around His neck swings a garland of flowers, His unique loveliness
Charming millions of cupids, such splendid beauty does He possess.
I worship Shyamasundara, with the moon locket on His chest,
Whose graceful threefold-bending form is eternally manifest;
His hands are adorned with the golden flute and jeweled ornaments,
And He always revels in pastimes of joy, with His loving confidants.

CHINTAMANI

Lotus-eyed flute song
If you can sing along,
Takes you to another land
Made of love not sand.
Where a desire tree
Made of chintamani,
Nestles o'er a jeweled seat
Humming bees and flowers sweet,
Birds of love fly above
Cuckoo soft and white dove—
Radha tastes the mellow bliss
Of her Lord Govinda's kiss,
Lovely gopis dance and sing
In the bushes whispering,
Cows and cowherds gather round
Swooning to the lovely sound.
Krishna steals the hearts of all
Who can hear His flutesong call,
Dance and sing in ecstasy
In Vrindavan wandering free.
Lotus-eyed flute song
If you can sing along,
Takes you to another land
Made of love not sand.

ANKLE BELLS

Softly tinkling through the vales and dells
Floats the sound of Krishna's ankle bells,
Mingling with the rush of waterfalls
And the cuckoo sings her morning calls.
Sunbeams spread their fingers through the boughs
Of the ageless trees that shelter cows,
Calves, and cowherd boys who dance and sing
Through the Vraja forest wandering.
Brilliant peacocks dance in ecstasy
Shyamasundar's lotus feet to see,
Dark blue rain clouds fill the amber sky
Over grasses green where Gopis cry—
Madly searching for a cowherd boy
Krishna Who has stolen all their joy,
Searching for His footprints on the ground,
Languishing to hear His flute song sound.

SHYAMASUNDAR

His eyes are like a lotus flower
Poised above a crystal pool.
His arms are long and filled with power
Like the moon His hands are cool.
Soft radiance surrounds His face
With forest flowers in His hair,
His body strong and filled with grace
Imparts a fragrance to the air.
With secret lips of corral red
And eyebrows arched like cupid's bow;
A peacock feather on His head
Above His garments' golden glow.
Surrounded by the forest creatures
Beside a gently flowing stream,
The moonlight playing on His features
Like a sweet enchanting dream.
He's standing there within our soul
The Lord we left so long ago,
To please and serve Him is our goal
His love is all we need to know.

CUPID'S SECRET

Vrindavan the source of all beauty and radiance,
With bowers of lotus, the seat of a jewel rare;
Secret garden enchanting where wanders in delicate dance—
Divine loving pair.
Soft moon beams of silver with nectar perfume the night air.
While peacocks like rainbows, and cuckoos sweet sing to enhance,
With garlands of ecstasy circling the bamboo lair;
And a distant flutesong evergreen hearts does entrance.
His crown at Her feet forest flowers in Her hair,
Attracting the heart of Cupid Their secret glance—
Divine Loving Pair.

GOLOKA VRINDAVANA

Vrindavana is such a wonderful place
Where bumble bees hum and songbirds sing,
While cowherd boys the monkeys chase
Across the hills their voices ring.
And the rushing sound of the waterfalls
Plays in the caves on Govardhana Hill,
Sweetly covering the crickets' calls
While the sounds of musical laughter spill—
Across a green and grassy field
Filled with white surabhi cows,
As rivers of milk they lovingly yield
And tears flow from their gentle brows;
Where desire trees' boughs touch the ground
In humble devotion offering their fruit,
And praying to hear the blissful sound
Of Shyamasundar's golden flute.
Goloka Goloka my heart's delight
Where colorful peacocks dance in joy,
And pretty Gopi damsels roam
In search of a blackish cowherd boy.
Goloka Goloka my hearts delight
Divine loving lotus with fragrant sweet,
Land of the endless full moon night
Of searching the woods for His lotus feet.
O let me be a speck of dust
Upon the path where He may dance,
To satisfy the milkmaid's lust
With nectar from His restless glance.

JAYA RADHE

O golden Radharani fairest maid
Wandering in a silent bamboo glade,
Like the pale and wanning crescent moon
Reflected on a shimmering lagoon.
Black, and moist with tears, Her restless eyes
Search everywhere, while night conceals Her sighs
And gently floats the sound of Her lament,
Eternal song of love's embodiment.
Trembling shoulders graced with forest flowers,
Move in separation through the bowers.
Her shining garment's highest artistry
Bedecked with glowing jewels of ecstasy,
An evolution of transcendent treasure
Covered by the blouse of angry pleasure—
Searching in the woodland and the heather
For a glimpse of Krishna's peacock feather.
O lovely Radharani golden ocean,
Dearmost gopi, queen of lotusland,
Eternal mother emblem of devotion
Please bless us with Your gentle loving hand.

AN INTIMATE CIRCLE

Heavenly blue-tinged
Bamboo flute-song,
Saffron kunkum
Nectar lake,
Full moon, sweet smile
Milkmaids laughing,
Sunshine starlight
Night opaque.
Swan song sunset
Azure angels,
Cuckoos peacocks
Bumblebees fly,
Lavender lotus
Lily soft white,
Indigo amethyst
Autumnal sky.
Glowing gopis
Queens of the land.
Airplanes showering
Flowers and laughter,
Languishing lovers
Lament for His hand.

RASA DANCE

Soft silver moonbeams fill the Autumn night
And twinkling stars bedeck the firmament,
With amethyst and pearls of cool delight
While glowing dancers in rare ornament—
Draw graceful circles amidst the fragrant flowers,
Sweet zephyrs bear the song of frenzied bees;
And black deer watch wide-eyed from sheltered bowers
Within the hollows of the whispering trees.
With peacock feather rainbow on His head
The gopi's hands upon His shoulders rest,
Enchanting flutesong through the night is spread
And on His feet the kunkum from their breast.
Govinda dances with the milkmaids fair,
And gently places flowers in their hair.

MONSOON

Gopal Krishna with the cowherds playing
Cows and calves on the meadow straying,
Gopi girls, bangles jangling, churning
Butter singing gaily songs and yearning.
Peacocks strutting under cloudy skies
Eyelids flutter over restless eyes,
Gopijanaballabha smiling slightly—
Thinking shyly of the dancing nightly.

NECTAR NIGHT

Selflessness relieves distress,
The gentle rain of happiness,
Puts out the burning fire of life,
Transports the soul beyond all strife.
Past starry night and cruel death,
For those who give their living breath,
Upon their lips the holy Name
In praise of He who loving came,
To them a store of bliss is known
And hidden worlds to them are shown—
Where love Supreme fills every eye,
Sweet jubilation fills the sky,
As dancing milkmaids and cowherd boys
Play in forests green with joys
Of bale and jack fruit, lily white,
And endless full moon nectar night—
Of dancing magic loving smiles
And gopi damsel's playful wiles.
They sport in lotus lakes with He
Whose glances taste of ecstasy,
An endless flowing stream of bliss,
Eternal dance, unending kiss.

THE GOLDEN AVATAR

In India five hundred years ago,
The Lord of all from out of boundless grace
Appeared His causeless mercy to bestow,
Upon a blind and suffering human race.

He came to save the lost souls from disgrace,
Appearing as the sages had foretold,
A gentle loving smile upon His face
And shining with the hue of purest gold.

Descending on this planet filled with woe,
A lonely island lost in outer space,
He sang and love of God began to flow
Like crystal water from a silver vase.

The rising moon was veiled in shadow lace,
A silken starlight mantle did enfold
The birth of He no darkness could erase,
And shining with the hue of purest gold.

The winter night was filled with His sweet glow,
His Lotus-flower, conch-shell, disk and mace
The power of the Holy Name would show,
The darkness of this winter age untrace;

And even benedict the low and base,
From neither man nor beast will He withhold—
His love will fill their hearts and hate replace,
And shining with the hue of purest gold.

Gouranga's brought His love to this dark place,
Just hear Him chanting, dance and sing behold—
The Holy Name within His heart's embrace,
And shining with the hue of purest gold.

PERHAPS I SHOULD CHANGE MY NAME

Perhaps I should change my name again
Or sail to a faraway land
And leave behind the memories
Without trying to understand.
It seems so long since the day we met
I'll never forget Your eyes
But where are You now when the night is long;
Were our promises only lies?
I can't get You out of my heart, I've tried
To love You is too much pain
I think You're becoming my God, O Lord
You are driving me insane.
And You know that I'll still be waiting
There's no hope left for me
Because everywhere I look Your eyes
Are all that I can see.

DEFEAT OF SPRING

As springtime danced across the mountains' shining
   golden peaks,
She dressed the hills in purple flowers from her
   blushing cheeks,
And kissed the breeze beneath the trees with lips
   of southern flame,
But even she could not outshine my passion for the
   holy name.
Her beauty, beauty still, but somehow different than
   before,
Like a little pool of water on the mighty ocean
   shore,
Or like the drops of water in the hoofprint of a
   cow—
Were not enough to tempt me from my sacred chanting
   vow.
For who once tasting nectar will accept the bitter
   draught,
And who while wandering free would not be sorry to
   get caught.
The clever serpent wears a rainbow jewel upon his
   head,
And smiling waits in darkness with unblinking eyes
   of red;
But feeling once Your lotus flower how can one
   forget?
Nor having once received Your mercy ever pay the
   debt,
O Shyamasundar cowherd boy, far lovelier than
   May,
You simply smiled and called my name, and stole my
   love away.

ECHO OF THE CONCH

Speak the message of the spirit,
Freedom loving men will hear it,
A sound that holy wars will launch,
The echo of Lord Krishna's conch.
Through the ether, down the ages
Sung by pure and holy sages,
Received by lost unhappy men,
A battle cry will rise again.
The banner raised within their heart,
Each man will pray to do his part
To serve the Lord with all his might,
To learn what's good and seek the light.
Defeating anger, greed and lust,
A government of love and trust,
Where people strive for higher goals,
Will rule a group of gentle souls—
Who serve the Lord in ecstasy
Without reward eternally,
Unbending men whose vows are staunch,
Will hear the echo of the conch.

SECOND-BIRTH

When dawn shook the stars with her bursting ray,
As burgeoning life shoots forth from earthly clay,
Night, rent asunder, split and fell from sight,
Banished by the rosy steeds of Helios' light.
This moment the soul is reborn and lives to die,
Second-birth, blessed moment, of breaking the tie
That binds the spirit to earth, the sharpened sword
Cuts illusion's nets and slays the savage horde
Of demons, the doubts that darkened the soul,
With chaos and turned her away from the goal.
Day blossoms, the lotus of youth faces East,
Drinks the golden nectar of hope, a feast,
In honour of Truth is announced to the few—
Who hunger and thirst on the path of the true
Living light streaming down from the beautiful face,
Of God out of sight and beyond outer space.
Hear the music celestial announcing His glory,
Heralding the arrival of His holy story:
O man, you were made in His glorious image,
Go on in your journey with new strength and courage,
For life leads you homeward, if only you will,
Hear the sweet voice within you so soft and so still,
Singing all through the night till the coming of dawn
Of His love in your heart, then when darkness is gone,
You will see Him and touch Him and fall at His feet,
And then you will know that your life is complete.

GOUR HARI

O Lord Your name a song so sweet
Is a whisper soft to eager ears,
Who crying seek Your soothing feet
And wash Your temple with their tears.

Your blackish eyes a lotus whorl
Attract the heart of a swan-like mind,
Who searching for a single pearl
A priceless treasure is blest to find.

Drink deep O men of piety
The nectar of the holy name,
Dive into the sea of ecstasy
Bow down before the cleansing flame.

Surrender all you falsely hold
And raise your arms in joyful dance,
With He Who shines like molten gold
Rise up and feel His loving glance.

O Lord Chaitanya fairest One
Your full moon rising in the skies,
Outshines the beauty of the sun
And fills with love our searching eyes.

REFUGEE

The forest echoes with a melody,
An early morning sylvan rhapsody,
A flute and lute in perfect harmony,
Like words combined in rhyming prosody.
The drifting clouds like waves of ebony,
Rejoice their thunder's rolling euphony,
Outpouring notes like teardrops watery
And treetops rustle with the symphony.
The peacocks fly with all their finery
Around the sheltered bower's reverie.
There twirling round and round in ecstasy
As if in some enchanting fantasy,
The pair entwined in dancing unity,
Like some great spinning spiral galaxy—
A loving dance of perfect purity
The two in one eternal deity,
Unfolding as an endless trilogy
Embracing all in their festivity.
Now having seen this gorgeous effigy
And hearing this delightful eulogy,
You'll understand my painful malady
And why I live my life a refugee.

FADED FLOWERS

O hear my Beloved I am waiting,
Where the moonbeams are kissing the dew,
In the darkness but anticipating
The time when Your promise comes true.
I searched near and far in the forest,
A place You'd be happy to lie,
Now I wait for Your footsteps my Dearest
But from crying my eyes have gone dry.
The flowers I picked have all faded,
Sweet lotus and jasmine so fine,
In the strands of my hair I had braided
While thinking of making You mine.
Where the curtains of creepers are waving,
There a waterfall flows down the hill,
Summer breezes increasing my craving
And the black deer stand perfectly still.
The swans all were sure You were coming,
The peacocks pretended to hear,
What the bumblebees sang in their humming
They all said You'd surely appear.
Still I sit in the night broken-hearted,
You may come if You ever get bored,
Here I sit where I was when we parted
In the night, in a forest, O Lord.

DARK AGE

A veil of evil hangs above the Earth,
Harbinger of night with weapons sharp,
The clarion of doom has taken birth
And crushing love, has broken heaven's harp.

Cement and steel where once the land was green,
And clouds of poison fill the threat'ning sky,
Where rain once fell and rainbows could be seen
The wells and hearts of men will soon be dry.

The clamour of machines has killed the birds,
Who used to fill the morning with their song,
And cruel men speak clever sounding words
To secretly confuse the right with wrong.

The rivers, fields and mountains of our lands
A birthright to our children from the Lord,
Have fallen into crooked leaders' hands
And no man dares to lift the sacred sword.

But listen man, as darkness gathers 'round,
One light still shines a pure and radiant flame,
Just breaking forth like sunrise is the sound—
of God, Who's come to save us by His name:

> Hare Krishna Hare Krishna
> Krishna Krishna Hare Hare
> Hare Rama Hare Rama
> Rama Rama Hare Hare.